Food Zone

All About
Meat and Fish

Vic Parker

QED Publishing

ESSEX CC LIBRARIES

30130 165207530

Copyright © QED Publishing 2009

First published in the UK in 2009 by
QED Publishing
A Quarto Group company
226 City Road
London EC1V 2TT

www.qed-publishing.co.uk

All rights reserved. No part of this publication may be reproduced, stored in a retrieval system, or transmitted in any form or by any means, electronic, mechanical, photocopying, recording, or otherwise, without the prior permission of the publisher, nor be otherwise circulated in any form of binding or cover other than that in which it is published and without a similar condition being imposed on the subsequent purchaser.

A catalogue record for this book is available from the British Library.

ISBN 978 1 84835 249 0

Author Vic Parker
Consultant Angela Royston
Project Editor Eve Marleau
Designer Kim Hall
Illustrator Mike Byrne

Publisher Steve Evans
Creative Director Zeta Davies
Managing Editor Amanda Askew

Printed and bound in China

Picture credits
(t=top, b=bottom, l=left, r=right, c=centre, fc=front cover)

Alamy Images 7br Guillen Photography/UW/Canada/Quebec, 15t Grant Heilman Photography/Larry Lefever, 15cr Vehbi Koca, 15b Bernhard Classen/Vario images, 19cr Alberto Paredes, 19b Tim Hill
Corbis 14cl C.Fleurent/Photocuisine
Dreamstime 13t Konstantin Karchevskiy
Getty Images 18b Dorling Kindersley
Photolibrary 9b Christina Peters, 14b Michael Krabs, 15cl Novastock Novastock
Rex Features 12b Garo/Phanie, 14cr Sipa Press, 19cl Image Source
Shutterstock 4tl Zaichenko Olga, 4tc Denis Dryashkin, 4tr Eric Isselée, 4bl Dmitrijs Mihejevs, 4br Tischenko Irina, 5tl Alexey Khromushin, 5tc JackF, 5tr G.Lancia, 5cl Guilu, 5cr Morgan Lane Photography, 5b Peter Baxter, 6l Zaichenko Olga, 6r Tischenko Irina, 6–7 Martine Oger, 7tl Dmitrijs Mihejevs, 7tr Mirrormere, 7bl Eric Isselée, 8t Cappi Thompson, 8bl Amfoto, 8bc, 8br Joe Gough, 9t Monkey Business Images, 11t (brazil nuts) Leonid Shcheglov, 11t (steak) Paul Cowan, 11c (salmon) Paul Cowan, 11b (chicken) Semenovp, 11bl Gerrit_de_Vries, 11br Norman Chan, 12t Tischenko Irina, 12c Ramon Berk, 13c Andrei Nekrassov, 13bl Tischenko Irina, 13br Alex Staroseltsev, 14t Zaichenko Olga, 18t Eric Isselée, 18c Eduard Kyslynskyy, 19t Lagui

Words in **bold** are explained in the glossary on page 22.

Contents

What are meat and fish?

Meat and fish are animal products that we can eat.

Meat includes beef, pork, lamb and poultry, such as chicken. Other animal products we can eat include fish and eggs. Meat, fish and eggs are all rich in **protein**, which is important to our health.

Chicken

Eggs

Lamb

Prawns

Fish

You will need

- 450 g small, cooked prawns, peeled
- 200 g mayonnaise
- 3 tbsp tomato ketchup
- 1 tbsp lemon juice
- An iceberg lettuce, chopped
- Mixing bowl
- Four small bowls

Make a... prawn cocktail

1 Mix the mayonnaise, ketchup and lemon juice in a bowl.

2 Mix the prawns into the sauce.

3 Put a handful of lettuce in each bowl.

4 Place the prawns and sauce mixture on top of the lettuce – and enjoy!

Seafood such as squid, crabs, lobsters, mussels and oysters are rich in protein, too.

Squid

Oysters

Mussels

Crab

Lobster

⇧ Seafood such as crabs and lobsters are types of shellfish.

5

Where do meat and fish come from?

Different types of meat and fish come from all over the world.

In some countries, people eat one kind of meat or fish more than any others. This is usually because it is farmed there.

North America

Atlantic Ocean

Pacific Ocean

South America

The United States eats and produces the most chickens in the world.

Salmon are fished in the Pacific Ocean. There are different types of salmon, including pink salmon and sockeye salmon.

Prawns live in waters around Iceland and Norway. Most of the catch is sold in Europe.

China produces the most chicken eggs in the world.

Asia

Snow crabs come from the Sea of Japan. Snow crabs live where the waters are very deep and cold.

Africa

Indian Ocean

Oceania

A lot of lamb is farmed in New Zealand. Much of it is eaten in Europe and Oceania.

How do we eat meat and fish?

We eat foods with protein, such as meat, fish and eggs, with most meals.

For lunch, you might eat some salmon fishcakes.

For breakfast, you could have scrambled egg on toast.

For dinner, you could have a chicken curry.

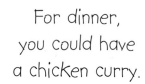

8

You will need

- 50 g sweetcorn
- 1 tbsp mayonnaise
- 1 small can of tuna in water, drained
- 15 g cheddar cheese, grated
- Wholegrain bread roll
- Salt and pepper
- Mixing bowl

Make a... tuna sweetcorn melt

1 Mix the sweetcorn, mayonnaise and tuna in the bowl with salt and pepper.

2 Ask an adult to cut the bread in half and spread the mixture on the roll.

3 Ask an adult to turn on the grill to high. Sprinkle the cheese over the tuna and grill until it has has melted. Enjoy!

Fish and shellfish can be cooked in many different ways, from grilled or fried to poached or barbecued. In Japan, fish and shellfish are often eaten raw with rice. This is called sushi.

⇧Some of the most popular ingredients in Japanese meals are fish and rice.

Why does your body use meat and fish?

Meat and fish contain protein. Your body needs protein, vitamins and minerals.

Fish contains protein, which your body uses to make hair, bones and other parts of the body.

Red meat, such as beef, contains **iron**, which helps to keep your blood healthy.

Meat such as chicken contains **zinc**, which helps the body to heal wounds.

Beef

Red meat, such as beef, is a good source of protein.

Brazil nuts

Brazil nuts contain protein and minerals, which your body needs to work properly.

Salmon

Fish such as salmon contains **omega 3**, which is good for your heart.

Chicken

White meat such as chicken, is low in fat, making it healthier than red meat.

Macadamia nuts

Eat a... macadamia nut

Macadamias are high in protein and have a sweet taste.

Fish

How are fish caught?

A lot of the fish we eat comes from the sea.

1

Fishing boats can stay out at sea for many weeks. They have all the equipment necessary to catch fish, and then freeze or tin it, too.

Fish that live deeper in the sea, such as sea bass, are caught by trawling. A boat drags a huge net through the water, catching everything in its path.

2a

Fish farmers raise fish in netted-off areas or huge outdoor tanks, especially to be sold for food. Common farmed fish include carp, trout and salmon.

2b

3

Fish from farms and the sea are either taken fresh, frozen or tinned to shops and supermarkets.

Trout

Food news

Nearly half of all the fish we eat are farmed rather than caught in the wild.

Salmon

Eggs

Chicken

How are chickens and eggs farmed?

The chickens and eggs we eat come from different farms.

1 Hens lay eggs in nests inside hen houses. On chicken farms, the eggs hatch into chicks.

If the eggs hatch, the chicks are kept indoors. Special heat lamps keep them warm.

2

3 On free-range poultry farms, chicks are allowed outdoors when they are about two weeks old.

4 When the chickens are more than 20 weeks old, they are taken to a **slaughterhouse**.

The chickens are then sold fresh or frozen in shops and supermarkets.

5

6 Egg farms produce the eggs we eat. The farmer collects the eggs, or they fall onto a **conveyor belt**.

A code showing the date is printed onto each egg. Then the eggs are packed into boxes and taken to shops.

7

★ Ask an adult ★
Always ask an adult to help you make the recipe and get all the ingredients and equipment ready. Remember to wash your hands before you start.

Make some paella

Paella is a Spanish recipe that includes different types of meat, such as chicken, and fish.

You will need

- 2 tbsp olive oil
- 1 onion, sliced
- 110 g of chicken fillet, diced
- 1 tsp turmeric
- 300 g long grain rice
- 1 litre fish or chicken stock
- 200 g frozen peas
- 400 g white fish, such as pollock, diced
- 1 lemon, cut into wedges
- Salt and pepper
- Deep frying pan
- Wooden spoon

1

Ask an adult to heat the oil in the pan, then fry the onion for three minutes.

Add the chicken and fry for five minutes until it is golden brown.

2

16

3 Stir in the turmeric and rice, then pour in the stock. Bring it to the boil and simmer for 15 minutes, stirring occasionally.

Add the fish and cook for five minutes. Add the frozen peas and cook for another five minutes.

4

5 Add a pinch of salt and pepper and serve with wedges of lemon.

Lamb

How is lamb farmed?

A lamb is a young sheep. Lambs are often raised on farms in hilly areas.

1 In autumn, the sheep farmer lets male sheep, or rams, live with the ewes, or female sheep.

At the end of February, the ewes are taken down to the farm buildings. During spring, each ewe gives birth to one or two lambs.

2

18

3 The lambs stay in barns for a few days. Then they may go to the fields with the ewes.

When the lambs are three to four months old, many of them are taken to a slaughterhouse.

4

5 Some of the meat is sold to factories and made into different food products. The rest is taken to shops and supermarkets.

Food news

Lamb is eaten all over the world. It may be made into shepherd's pie in Britain, and lamb **kebabs** in the Middle East.

Shepherd's pie

Lamb Kebab

★ Ask an adult ★
Always ask an adult to help you make the recipe and get all the ingredients and equipment ready. Remember to wash your hands before you start.

Make fish dippers

Use fish and egg to make this fun and tasty dish.

You will need

- 400 g of white fish, such as hake, cut in strips
- 120 g breadcrumbs in a bowl
- 1 egg, beaten, in a bowl
- 100 g plain flour in a bowl
- 2 tbsp vegetable oil
- Non-stick frying pan
- Small bowl of Ketchup

1

Take a strip of fish and roll it in the bowl of flour until it is lightly coated.

2 Dip the floury fish into the bowl of egg mixture until it is lightly coated.

3 Dip the fish into the bowl of breadcrumbs. Repeat stages one to three with all the fish strips.

Ask an adult to fry the strips in oil for 5–10 minutes, turning them over once or twice until the breadcrumbs are golden brown.

4

5 Wash your hands then serve your fish dippers with a small bowl of tomato ketchup.

Glossary

Conveyor belt
A constantly moving strip of material that carries objects along from one place to another.

Iron
A mineral that keeps your blood system healthy.

Kebab
Meat that is cooked on a metal or wooden stick.

Omega 3
A type of fat found in some fish, nuts and plants.

Protein
A substance found in foods such as red meat, fish, poultry, pulses and eggs that helps your body to grow and stay healthy.

Slaughterhouse
A building where animals are taken to be killed for food.

Zinc
A mineral found in foods such as chicken that helps to keep many parts of the body healthy, such as the immune system.

Notes for parents and teachers

- With the children, look at pictures of a variety of foods and pick out which ones are protein foods. Identify which animal each of the foods come from.

- In many countries, people keep chickens, goats and other animals to provide food for their families. Talk about how this is different from going to the shop to buy food produced on large farms.

- Talk about why our bodies need protein to stay healthy and how much we should eat every day.

- Discuss how to make healthier protein choices, such as fish or meat with a lower fat content, or methods of cooking that use less oil, such as grilling or steaming.

- Explain why people might be vegetarian or vegan, for example, ethical reasons, dietary reasons or religious reasons. Introduce the concept of vegetable protein and show some foods that are good sources, such as pulses, nuts, seeds, soya products, cereals, eggs, milk, cheese and yoghurt.

- Talk about how we might use different types of protein in cooking. Make an international protein cookbook with recipes and pictures from around the world.

Index